MY FAVORITE A

GROUNDHOGS

Victoria Marcos

xist Publishing

Table of Contents

My favorite animals are groundhogs. Would you like to learn about them?

Groundhogs are also called woodchucks. They are the largest members of the squirrel family.

They can be found in most of central and eastern United States and in parts of Alaska and Canada.

Adult males weigh around 13 pounds and are an average of 20 inches long.

Groundhogs spend most of their time underground in complex burrow systems.

They dig as far as six feet underground and as much as 20 feet in length.

Each burrow even has its own bathroom.

Groundhogs eat a lot all summer long.

In October, they retreat to their underground burrows and sleep until spring, living on their body fat.

While hibernating, the groundhog's heart rate slows down, and its body temperature is barely warmer than the temperature inside the burrow.

Do You Remember?

Groundhogs are a member
of what family?

Check and see if
you're right at the
end of this book!

Groundhogs eat about 1/3 of their weight every day in grasses and plants as well as fruits and tree bark.

Gardeners find groundhogs to be destructive.

They can destroy a large area while feeding during the summer in preparation for hibernation.

Groundhogs drink very little water. Most of their liquids come from wet leaves.

Do You Remember?

How much do groundhogs eat each day?

Check and see if you're right at the end of this book!

Groundhogs hibernate. They enter deep sleep in October and don't come out of their dens until early spring.

In the spring, females give birth to about a half dozen newborns. They will stay with their mother for several months.

Groundhogs are mostly solitary animals.

They work together to protect each other.

They communicate with one another using high-pitched screams to warn each other of danger.

Groundhogs are good climbers and swimmers. This helps them to escape less-skilled predators.

Do You Remember?

How do groundhogs warn each other of danger?

Check and see if you're right at the end of this book!

Groundhogs are very clean.
This keeps them safe from insects
and disease.

Groundhogs are resistant to the
plague which sometimes wipes out
large numbers of wild animals.

What's your favorite thing about Groundhogs?

Glossary

Burrow: a hole or tunnel dug by a small animal as its home

Den: The home of an animal

Hibernate: To sleep through the winter

Plague: A contagious disease that often causes death

Predators: Animals that eat other animals.

Resistant: preventing or working against

Solitary: alone

Published in the United States by Xist Publishing
www.xistpublishing.com
PO Box 61593 Irvine, CA 92602

Did You Remember?

Answers:
Question #1:
Squirrel
Question #2:
1/3 of their weight
Question #3:
Using high-pitched screams

Made in the USA
Coppell, TX
13 May 2023

16803527R00024